Arirang

Akila

BookLeaf Publishing

India | USA | UK

Presentation by *BookLeaf Publishing*

Web: www.bookleafpub.com

E-mail: info@bookleafpub.com

ISBN: 9789363312821

First edition 2024

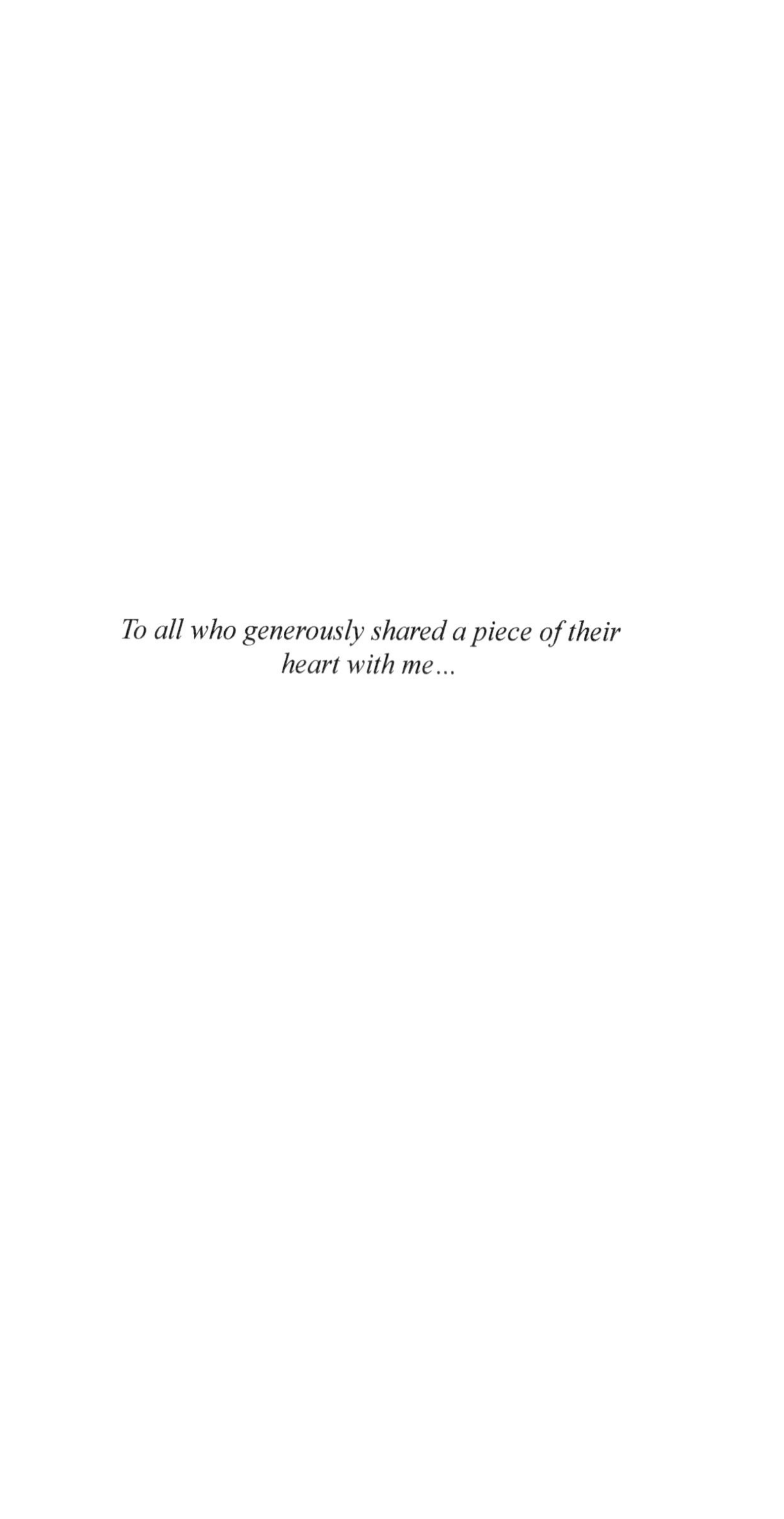

*To all who generously shared a piece of their
heart with me…*

ACKNOWLEDGEMENT

I exist as a compilation of your memories and the generosity of your spirit.

Appa and Amma - You are my beginning and my everything. My love for you knows no bounds!!

My family - You are my roots, my wings, and my nest. I am richer because I have you. You all inspire me to be a better person every day.

SA - When you say, "On days when you don't have enough love for yourself, I will love you more." You are my conscience and my light.

HS - What's more than your friendship! You inspire me every day.

Muses - You are the ink of my soul and the drive in my pen.

PREFACE

Me, You have no clue!
You! You wake me from my depths,
And ask me to live,
Hope that I learn to Be.
To smile, to fret,
To carry the forlorn hope
That someday
I can make you see me.

Day & Night

It'd be fine, they said.
You'd live, they said.

An off switch! A past!
Humble in its rubble, preserved in its infancy.
A freeing flight without an anchor, broken in its spirits!
Hope in its embers, aching for a home.

If what then was a fantasy, what then of now?
Little stones, many left unturned.

Brilliant reflection of 'something' that stood in the sun,
Cooling beams of moonlit memories.

In a constant confluence of 'almosts' and
'never-haves,'
Not bright in its glamour, but stronger in its
love.
A new dream will bloom, they never said.
A willful shadow will follow, they never
warned.

To reach unto you is my living breath

I wake up daily after a life with you
Dress up in case I see you.
My eyes search for you in every crowd,
Holding hands with empty air - isn't that odd?
Distance is a mere illusion.
I just heard you call me!

Every time you go home, you go home; you take
a piece of me—a piece of me.
Every time you come back home, come back
home; you take my peace - you take my peace
from me.

A poor man's dream of paradise!
Impossible scents born of my imagination.
I am screaming for your recognition

From beyond the camera lens.
Loving you is like chasing horizons,
A melody transcending time and hope.

I am just a fangirl
Of your life, of our perfect life.
Our journey and all that I rewrite.
The heart knows what it wants—
That one day, this lyric may find its music!

Sunday

In the rush and hustle, I slowly whittle,
Day by day in the grind.
Trophies and baggage
Brings balance and debts.
No time for kind words or a soft kiss.
Fear I lost the I, the Me, and the other three.

Now I have gentle dreams —
Mellow mornings and dewy memories,
Slow walks by the lakes,
Picnics and passion in the shade,
Stories with crickets by the fireside,
Rocking to sleep like curtains in the sea wind.

The best thing ever stolen:
Lazy Sundays with you,
To be forever and ever and ever.

Perceiving the shadow

Striking incoherence,
Plucking at disconnected chords,
Some gentle breezes
Tell tales of old fragrance—
Fanning the glowing embers
Lying just beneath,
Piercing the strong veils, and
Stinging at the soul's mirror -
It makes the pain ooze out.
For, losing a dear
Is seldom forgotten.
But blinking back, and
Concealing the wounds within,

Dropping the curtains down again,
We say of a gone scar
That is rarely remembered.

On my pillow

Seduction growing
in every caress,
aching for the forbidden secret,
bathed in exquisite agony.
During palpable silence,
in the blink of a second,
the world changes mode.
Like the breeze in the storm,
on its way out,
igniting the icicle.
Where one ends, another begins,
that the soul knows not.
A timeless continuum,
this primal innocence.

Dream of form in days of thought*

If you don't remember, then what was the point?
Of the beginnings and their ends,
Of greedy hearts and tender thoughts,
Of nights of moon and promises of stars,
Of baby dreams and solid grounds,
Of silent questions and answered kisses,
Of the taste of hunger and pleas for quiet,
Of stolen wishes and empty verses,
Of woes of joy and depths of faith,
Of washed-up desires and chosen poison,
Of tales of burdock, minnows, and elephants,
Of honest haunts and bloodied silence,
Of the short truth and longer shadow,
Of everything from here back to the start.
If you can't forget, then what was the point?

Dream a little wish

Give me a chance – I will show you how,
How you are missed.
Give me a glance – I will reverse the wilt
And stand tall once again.
Give me your song – I will wear it proud,
In my ring, around my name.
Give me your pride – I will teach you a thing or
two,
And hold you between heaven and hell
Give me your seed – I will grow her strong,
Full of sunshine and endless smiles!
Give me your prayers – I will chant them every
breath,
Wishing they all come true.
Give me your arms – I will lean on,
For you to lean in.

Give me your time – I shall be your slave!
Totus tuus ego sum!

Cinema: Life

I also live a reel life, while reeling in my own.
It's fun to roll with the slides. That
Offers a spectacular view of life;
Pictures of coherent moments.
I'm part of love; I witness war.
One day, I'm a beggar.
In the next, I'm God.
Some days are overwhelming, loud;
A party, a crowd.
While on others, I'm lazy;
Lonely and bored.
Staring at footprints
Left behind in their wake,
I live my life in my head.
Well, what do you expect?
I'm just an audience!

Mini Love Letters

I once held something dear.
As it walked away, caught its prints in snow.
Hid it between layers and years.
It grew as a tree of regret,
Only to be swayed by a simple "Hello!"
_^_

You lay on a haystack,
Staring at the moonlit expanse.
A million eyes wink at you.
In that glare, you miss my smile.
Somewhere far away, a star jumps to its death.
..*_ _*..

I hid my love in time,
Dark and clandestine,
Unchanging, peripheral.
No Void. No Null.
_ *_ *

I'm a word in the missive,
You are the dream in my open eyes.
I'm your fourth wall,
You are my elephant-in-the-room.

It is what it is

We are the chances we didn't take.
We are the words that we didn't speak.
We are the turns that we missed.
We are the truths we dismissed.
We are the energy we did waste.
We are the questions we didn't chase.
We are the remains of who we aren't.
We are the answer to what could have been!

Celebration of Life

Have you wondered,
Why is there sadness when the world wants
happy?
Why is there fighting when peace is holy?
Why is there evil when all was intended to be
good?
Why is there failure when all we need is only
success?

Once,
I sowed a seed;
It gave fruit in need.
In the rain, it danced,
High and wide, it fanned.

In twinkling light, it glowed,
Beautiful branches in the air flowed.
Soon fate played a part—and made us part.
My toil was brought down with axes huge,
Now where will I take refuge?
Even the heavens cried,
But I could only sigh!
The next day dawned bright,
Amidst the ruins came a new life.

I realized,
Every storm causes a blow,
To inform a new start comes a rainbow.
For every night, there is a day,
To lighten up the darkness, comes a ray.
Life involves love and hate,
Acceptance and rejection. One comes
To educate us about the other.

In all that divide-
I need to
Celebrate the gift called life!

I'm wondering, are you my best friend?

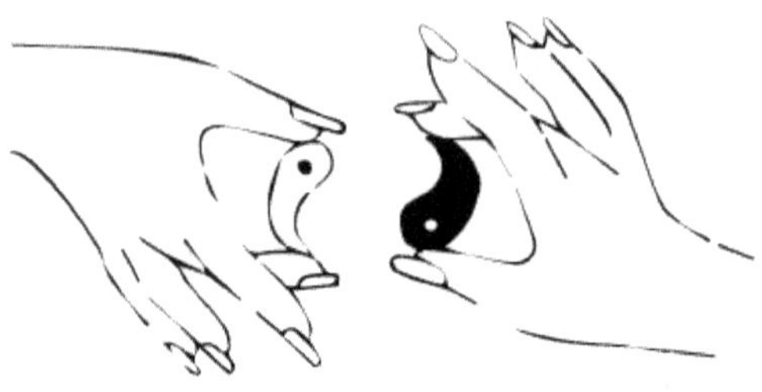

Slave to his song, she was,
A stranger he was to her.
Strumming her feelings with words,
Singing as if he knew her...as
Though had lived with her, in her past,
Reading her every thought,
Her heart's unfinished letters,
Her soul's deepest desire.
He lived, not realizing her presence,
She, in agony, that he was around.

The song of friendship…
In the rhyme of words,
'You are my four-leaf clover.' Such cliché!
Which she treasured and wanted more.
The tune of dearness…
In the rhythm of care,

'I wish I could stay with you,'
Which she possessed and wanted more.
He, a dream in reality,
But a reality in dream.

The incentives come at an expense,
Not for the rainbow,
But for the sunshine she yearns.
He may be miles and smiles away,
Yet, in a phrase, in a song, in a scent, he lives,
So close, very close, that it makes her gasp for
breath.
The moral he explained,
A reason to smile, even now.

She wants to hear him say it,
Only once…just once!
Desperately wants it to be a reality.
She is prepared to wait till eternity…

Never belonged..,

Preserved a single dream.
Such perfection, it felt so right,
The imprint on a fragile heart.
Unresolved, unrequited,
I contemplated day & night,
To nurture safe, under eyelid,
Or, instead, under rocks to hide.
I chose the latter. Echoes in the dark.
Unspoken words, fragile heart, doth break
When, mind's eye, with eloquence, reverberates.
Repress, forget, I tried with might,
The rocks crushed harder.

What do I do? Now I've got
A million broken smiles to worry.
But are diamonds ever brittle?

Long longed for

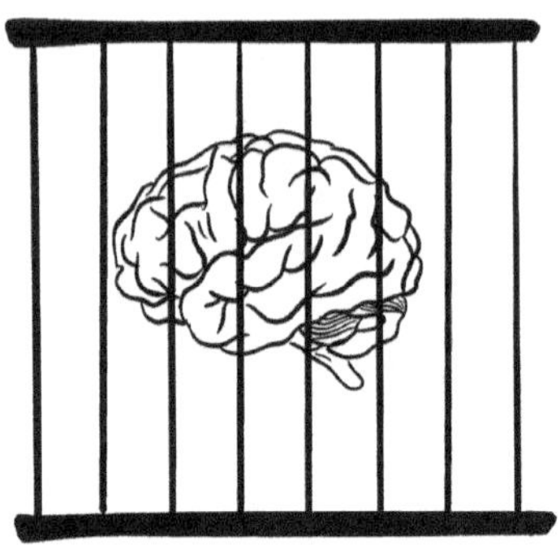

Oh, life-burdened traveler,
Walking the paths of destiny.

When it gets too loud,
Hang up the saddle,
Rest your weary head,
On dry grass and rough grounds,
Call on your siren.

Let it spin memories,
Of silk satin and soft cotton linen,
Incense and rubies and myrrh.
Where you're always chosen.
Always her first.

Smells of burnt toast and tea—
Life gets in the way.

Grass is wet,
Rain and something like despair.
She, still travels,
The ember in frozen snow.

When your hope stands in the shadow of fear,
Dreams don't bother
With light or dark.

Life, Thank you for humoring us.

What I lack in experience,
I make up for in my imagination.
What I lack in imagination,
I make do with anxiety.
What escapes my anxiety,
I make up by overthinking.
When it's an active mind and empty eyes,
I make it loud with insistent inner dialogue.
When saids and unsaids are heavy,
I make friends with my handsome demons.
When every breath becomes a sigh,
I make up sleep with a restless promise, that
I will do all this again tomorrow.
I never learn from experience.

Sugar is real tonight

Today,
Today I am wearing the same smile you left me!
We are,
We are the two without ever a goodbye.

Oh, how!
And how,
We were.
We were in love!
In love!
With ourselves, being in love.

When we are old and grey,
Sometimes lose focus and slide down a high.
Just on a time like today,
Can we slip back to who we used to be?

When I,
I was in love with my idea of love.
When you,
You, in love with your dream of an ideal.

Who knows! Maybe we will be ready
To be who we could never be.

Need for latibulation

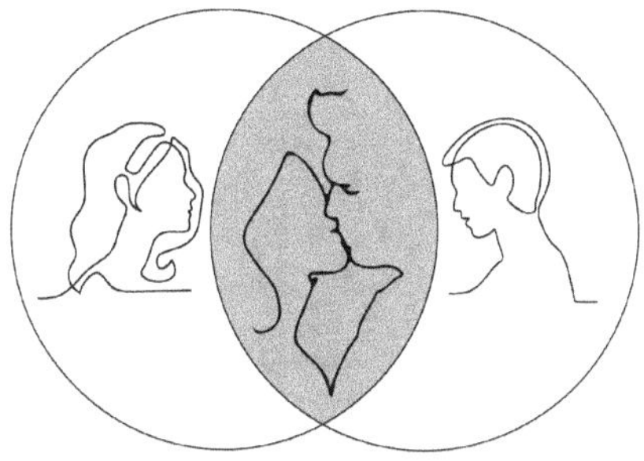

You are taught to handle this with care.

You think it's a start.
You think you can hang on to that spark,
All-seeing but never seen,
Loyal yet unrecognized,
Needed but never really wanted,
Recognizable in its insistency,
But annoying in its consistency.

With a braveness that comes only to the reckless,
Always low density and high intensity,
HOPE flares like an unwanted acne on an
important day.

Are you worthy of it?
Is it worthy for you?

I love being in love with you

...a year since they parted.

The eyes that made her feel like a woman,
The words that teased her as if she were a child,
The smile, which she longed for, wanting more,
The name, that became her identity,
The personality that awakened all her senses…

The touch, which felt like the gentle caress of
breeze,
The shoulders, where she wanted to lie all her
life,
The arms, which she wished would always hold
hers,
The love, which made her dream about
togetherness,
The secrecy, which made her inner self glow…

The night had not dawned,
The dreams still undreamt,
All that she wished...
Was all that she had…

The reality scared her heart,
Then depression engulfed her being,
The revelation buried in her thoughts,
The loss in the game made her quit.

May her love rest in peace!

(Un)conditional..

If I can just lie there and listen to you breathe in
sleep and feel comforted, then I will never be
lost.

If I can just read your eyes and understand the
words and their meaning, then there will be no
more silent moments.

If I can just hold you tight in my arms and still
feel not-close-enough, then that's where my
home is.

If I can accept your kisses as gifts, then I will
never be poor.

If I can love you the way you love me, then I'm
truly blessed.

If I can let you fall asleep on my shoulders, then
my prayers may never go unanswered.

If I can just connect with you through thoughts,
then no distance is a big one.

If I can just talk the language of love, which
only you can feel and reciprocate, then I'll have
everything I will ever want.

If I can find, in your love, the sunshine to expel
my winter mist, then I will truly believe in love.

Black rose!

Accepting it is ripping the heart out.
Tears, not dissolving the memories..
Pretentiously trying to exude happiness,
but the truth stalking every minute—like
a thorn.
An open cut!

Maybe destiny is not a hoax..
Blaming that to ease the pain..
Soothingly affirming to the soul,
there is still more to life— like
in a rose.
Just a scar!

In the heart and mind,
emotions are like the seasonal change.
At the start, new and pleasant. Enjoy!

Some days cloudy and gray. Doubt!
Rain and light. Revel!
Then calm! Move away!
Thunderstorm. Deny!
Now the thoughts—
Slush! Murky!
All in the same heart and mind.

Only deafening silence reigns.
But, inside—roaring voices,
flashing memories! Conflicts -
between own dimensions.

Making desperate attempts, to
loosen the wrought iron grip..
Break free of the shackles that are
tying the hands opening the gift.
Evade the conventional bonds.
Eluding the feeling of guilt.
Run from the pressing thoughts.
Float around—and
move far, far away from the crowd.

But wherever I go,
even in the darkness of the dark,
unfortunately,
'I' am still there.

Birth

Memoirs of a Promise:
On a bright blue Tuesday,
I was conceived—
of tales of "Robin" and the like.
And assuredly, I became.
Since then, it's been
weeks a many.
Feels shorter than one,
For the prospect
was rather pleasant.
I saw no summons,
Yet, I held belief.
Now, I, the Promise, surmise

was on water writ.
Oye, idle Promiser,
do, give a push,
and claim your deliverance.
The ball and the court are yours~